165

C000220638

Copyright © Rupa & Co 2002
Text © V. Gangadhar 2002

Published in 2002 by

Rupa & Co

7/16, Ansari Road, Daryaganj
New Delhi 110 002

Sales Centres:
Allahabad Bangalore Chandigarh Chennai
Dehradun Hyderabad Jaipur Kathmandu
Kolkata Ludhiana Mumbai Pune

Photographs courtesy: Atmanaban and Kalki Kannan

Cover & Book Design by
Arrt Creations
45 Nehru Apts, Kalkaji, New Delhi 110 019
arrt@vsnl.com

Printed in India by
Gopsons Papers Ltd.,
A-14 Sector 60
Noida 201 301

M.S. Subbulakshmi

THE VOICE DIVINE

V. Gangadhar

Rupa & Co

CONTENTS

CHAPTER ONE

Personal Encounters

For long, Indian classical music was identified with the North Indian *gharanas,* while Carnatic music remained a regional passion. This picture changed with M.S. Subbulakshmi, the golden-voiced singer from the city of Madurai. Her genius and efforts popularised Carnatic music all over India and abroad.

For more than 60 years, 'MS' dominated classical music in the country, performing at five or six *kacheris* (concerts) a month. Music was a passion for her, linked to *bhakti*. She had over 2,500 songs as part of her repertoire. Nearly 300 of her concerts were

Performing at a 'Kacheri'

organised for charity and collected more than Rs. 3 crores for schools, hospitals, cultural centres and religious institutions. In fact, MS personified the *bhakti* cult and often stressed there could be no music without devotion.

There was something wonderful, almost divine, in her appearance too. She wore the choicest of silk sarees, and diamonds sparkled from her ears and nose. People caught their breath and whispered among themselves, '*Devi madhiri irrukanga*' (she resembles a goddess).

Meera

The impact of the 'devi cult' became more pronounced after the release of the film *Meera* in 1945, where MS played the lead role of the Rajput queen who offered her soul to Lord Krishna. The movie was suffused with the overwhelming presence of the heroine, her exquisite beauty, devotion to Lord Krishna and the sweetness of its musical score. One of the four films she starred in, *Meera* became a rage. Everyone was humming its songs like *Katrinile Varum Geetam* (The melody carried by the breeze).

The Tamil and Hindi versions of *Meera* made Subbulakshmi a national figure. Presidents, prime ministers, envoys, industrialists and media stalwarts came under her spell. There was magic in her voice. She was invited to sing before a select audience at the United Nations in New York. If music could unite the world and bring it peace, this was it. MS began to be recognised as one of the greatest singers in the world and was fast becoming a legend.

For most people, Subbulakshmi was like a goddess — to be worshipped from a distance. She never talked to the media. The talking, if any, was done by her husband, T. Sadasivam, who efficiently managed her career. But I had the privilege of meeting and talking to MS in Chennai on September 10, 1998, a few days before her 82nd birthday. A life long MS fan, I had been haunted by her incredibly sweet and haunting song, *Malaipozhudhinile Oru Naal* (One evening).

The Kotturpuram (a Chennai suburb) bungalow where MS lives is a place of pilgrimage for music lovers. Visitors drop in at all times to have a *darshan* and seek her blessings. A diabetic for several years, she is looked after by Atmanaban, who served Sadasivam earlier. Sadasivam died in 1997 and MS has stopped performing in public.

Jawaharlal Nehru speaking at a benefit recital by MS

There is a feeling of history on entering her bungalow. The walls of the front room are full of framed photographs – MS in the company of national and international leaders including Gandhiji, Jawaharlal Nehru, Sardar Patel, the Mountbattens, famous musicians, her own gurus, composers, religious heads and a large picture of her mother and guru, Shanmukhavadivu. Tanpuras and veenas are placed at strategic corners. This was not just a home, but a temple for music. MS was sitting on the bed, her head covered with a scarf. She looked up, smiled and asked us to come closer. The face had lost none of its beauty and radiance. The voice was as soft and enchanting as ever.

To start with Subbulakshmi made it clear that despite having several gurus off and on, she was deeply indebted to her mother Shanmukhavadivu, a famous veena artiste, and found nothing wrong in her husband managing her career. MS was reluctant to

Sadasivam and Subbulakshmi

discuss controversial issues concerning music nor was she prepared to make a comparison between the singers of the past and the present.

"Look, I am not an expert in music," she confided with disarming frankness. "These days I do not listen to music all that much and cannot pass judgement on today's singers." But she made one point clear, about the *bhakti* element in music. "There cannot be any Indian music without the *bhakti rasam*," she emphasised. If music was a beautiful, fragrant flower, the beauty was its musical quality. The fragrance came from the content of the song, which ought to be *bhakti*.

The rich tradition in Carnatic music, offered plenty of scope for variety. As she mastered other languages, her repertoire increased dramatically. MS pointed out that most of today's musicians tended to adopt a low *shrudhi*, opting for one or one-and-a-half *kattai* (pitch). This was after the introduction of the microphone and the singers' over-reliance on it. According to MS, music was more natural without using the microphone. She sang without a microphone before huge audiences of nearly 3,000 people at Mumbai's Shanmukhananda Auditorium. Her voice reached every corner of the hall.

K.S.Raghunathan, veteran sound recordist with HMV, explained how MS was very particular during recordings. "She was worried when the accompanists made slight mistakes and felt they were her fault," he pointed out. She never compromised on quality, would not agree to any 'adjustments'. When Subbulakshmi finally said, 'okay', everyone breathed more freely, knowing the recording would be without mistakes.

CHAPTER TWO

The Early Years

The rulers of the ancient Pandya kingdom in Tamil Nadu have enriched the capital city of Madurai with the best in Tamil literature, music, architecture and the fine arts. The Meenakshi Temple and the Thirumalai Naicker Mahal are magnificent testimonies to the skill of the sculptors. No cultural or religious pilgrimage to Tamil Nadu would be complete without a visit to this great city.

In the same Madurai, at the home of veena artiste Shanmukhavadivu, located at the Upper Hanumantharayan Temple street, the dawn was always greeted with exquisite Carnatic music.

Tanpuras, veena, violin and the mridangam, played together created a wonderful symphony and made the passers-by halt a bit, nod their heads in appreciation and move ahead. The house was a temple of music. As women from the neighbouring homes stepped out to create intricate *kolams* (Rangoli) they were greeted with music.

Shanmukhavadivu belonged to the *Devadasi* community, dedicated to serving God through song and dance. Her family boasted of great musicians and music lovers. Her mother, Akkammal, was a noted violin player. The father, Swaminathan, was a music lover and patron of the fine arts. Shanmukhavadivu wanted to be a singer but lacked the voice for it, and had to switch over to playing the veena. Coached by great *vidwans*, she started performing solo from the age of fifteen. In those days, veena players had no accompanists and had to be prepared for solo recitals lasting four to five hours.

Veena artiste Shanmukhavadivu, who nurtured her daughter's early love of music

13

Subbulakshmi

Shanmukhavadivu married Subramania Iyer, one of the leading lawyers of Madurai and a lover of Carnatic music. Encouraged by his support, her fame as a veena player spread far and wide. Music lovers flocked to listen to her *kacheris* and showered expensive gifts on her. A big admirer of Shanmukhavadivu was 'Veenai' Dhanammal, acknowledged to be the best in the field.

M. S. Subbulakshmi was born in this temple of music on September 16, 1916. Her elder brother Shaktivel played the mridangam while the younger sister, Vadivambal, following her grandmother, took to the violin. MS was known by the pet name, 'Kunjamma' (The Little One), and naturally, she quickly absorbed the musical environment at home. At every possible opportunity the sisters sat down for *sadhakam*. Kunjamma sang, her sister played the violin, and sometimes her brother accompanied them on the mridangam. Kunjamma was fascinated by the mridangam, listened to her brother's playing avidly and soon became a fairly good player herself.

The daughter was keenly interested in her mother's mastery of the veena. Her earliest interest in music was focussed on the *ragas*. As the mother played and rehearsed constantly, Kunjamma absorbed the best in music by listening and humming with the veena. When noted

Young MS after a recital

sangeeta vidwans dropped in at home to sing and discuss music, the small girl was an avid listener.

The music-filled home was near the Meenakshi temple. Whenever the deity was taken in a procession through the main streets, the *nadaswaram* (wind instrument played in temples) players stopped near the house and played their best to win the approval of Shanmukhavadivu. Kunjamma listened, without missing a single beat. The mother, who had longed to be a singer, was determined that at least her daughter should excel in this field.

Vadivambal died too early to fulfil the rich promise she had shown. The mother now focussed on Kunjamma becoming a singer. After hearing Kunjamma sing, veena maestro Dhanammal told the mother, "Forget making Kunjamma a veena player. Listen to her divine voice, she is meant to be a singer." Now the search for a *guru* began and the choice fell on a well-known local musician, Srinivasa Iyengar. On an auspicious day, coconuts were broken, planetary positions were checked and Kunjamma was initiated into a proper study of Carnatic music.

The lessons continued till the girl had mastered *alankaram*, *kirtana* and *varnam*. Since Srinivasa Iyengar had taught the pupil everything he knew, Shanmukhavadivu decided to teach Kunjamma herself. As the 'teacher-mother' played the veena, the

Shanmukhavadivu Lalithangi (M.L. Vasanthakumari's mother) MS and Saraswathi Bai. Picture taken in 1935, when MS gave a concert.

daughter sang with her. She accompanied her mother to all the *kacheris* and never suffered from stage fright. Singing was in her blood, it came so naturally. Several years later, delivering the presidential address at the Madras Music Academy, MS paid glowing tributes to her mother and guru: "What little knowledge of music I possess today, I owe in the first instance to my mother, the late Shanmukhavadivu of Madurai. Both as my mother and music teacher, I bow before her and pray for her soul force to be with me all the time."

Kunjamma gave her first 'public concert' when she was eight or nine. How did it happen? The audience sat engrossed at a veena concert in the local Sethupati High School. Shanmukhavadivu looked around for the small figure who usually sat next to her. On that day, Kunjamma had left the dais to have some fun and play near the hall. One of the organisers, deputed by the mother, brought her back to the stage. Kunjamma sat next to her mother with the usual reverential attitude. Wiping beads of sweat from the child's forehead, Shanmukhavadivu whispered to her, "Come on, sing the *Anandaja* song". Without any fuss or self-consciousness, Kunjamma began to sing. Her voice rose strong, sweet and clear. The diction was perfect, every word had the right stress and intonation. The audience burst into applause and congratulated the mother and daughter after the performance.

Years later, MS recollecting her first 'concert' said, "At mother's bidding, I sang a couple of songs. I was too young to understand the smiles and the cheers. In fact, I was thinking more of returning to the mud where I had been playing!"

Kunjamma's father, Subramania Iyer, was equally interested in his daughter's career. A true *rasika* and *bhaktha*, he organised *Ramnavami* festivals with pujas, concerts and processions. He lifted his young daughter and placed her near the idol of Lord Rama when it was taken around the city in the traditional chariot. And at every single opportunity, he made the child sing.

Years later, MS laughingly remembered her appearance at her debut, "A side parting in thick curls pressed down with lots of oil, a huge dot covering most of the forehead, the half-saree pinned to the puffed blouse with a long brooch and longer safety pin, ear drops, nose rings and bangles of imitation gold. Oh, the long plait was tied with a strip of banana stem! A stage performance also meant pinning rows of medals on the shoulder."

When Kunjamma was ten, Shanmukhavadivu was invited to Madras to record some of her veena numbers. She took the child along because there could be more opportunities for her in the big city.

For the recording company, Shanmukhavadivu was a big star, but they were taken aback when the mother asked if it would be possible to record a song or two sung by her 10-year-old daughter.

Kunjamma, meanwhile, was intrigued by the gramophone records. She would roll a piece of paper into the shape of a 'speaker' and sing into it for hours. Now the game became real. But without any self-consciousness, Kunjamma sang a *bhajan* on Lord Muruga,

Maragatha Vadivum, Sengadhir Velum. The gramophone company people were astonished at the young girl's confidence and the resonant sweetness of her voice. Released as a twin record, featuring both mother and daughter, *Maragadha Vadivum* was a sell out.

Back in Madurai, Kunjamma began to sing regularly with her mother in her veena concerts. The response from listeners was electric. They could not distinguish who was better, the mother or the daughter! Shanmukhavadivu, watching the progress and growing self confidence of Kunjamma with delight, began to think of launching her daughter in solo concerts. This was a major step forward in any singer's career and required careful planning.

The girl was now past the 'Kunjamma' stage of her life. Subbulakshmi's first solo public concert was in Madurai. She was around 15. The *kacheri* was a big hit, both with the audience and music critics. The arrival of a new star in the world of Carnatic music was hailed by music lovers and soon Subbulakshmi began to receive invitations from Tiruchi, Ramanathapuram, Tirunelveli, Thanjavur and Chettinad, all bastions of Carnatic music.

The recording companies were not far behind. They besieged her with requests for recordings. *Nagumomo, Evarymada, Ini Enna*

Pechu were some of Subbulakshmi's earliest recordings. *Everymada*, a Thyagayya composition in *Raga Kambhoji*, became such a rage that the singer was labelled as '*Everymada MS*'. She was now introduced to the audiences as 'Kokila Ghana M.S.Subbulakshmi'.

Subbulakshmi was slowly getting recognised in the big league of Carnatic musicians. Eager to learn more, the young singer learnt *kirtanams* from *vidwans* like Ariyakudi Ramanuja Ayyangar, Musiri Subramania Iyer and Semmangudi Srinivasa Iyer. MS entered the world of Carnatic music when it was blessed with several 'stars' like Ariyakudi, Chembai Vaidyanatha Iyer, Maharajapuram Viswanatha Iyer, Chittoor Subramania Pillai and G.N.Balasubramaniam.

Opportunities to display her talent at concerts came thick and fast for MS. On January 1, 1932, she took the place of the indisposed Ariyakudi before the prestigious Madras Sangeeta Sabha. Could the 16-year old be an adequate substitute for the doyen of Carnatic music before such a discerning audience? The answer came very quickly. MS enthralled the audience with *kirtanams*, *varnams*, a delectable range of *ragam thanam pallavi* and *tukkadas* (lighter numbers). The *kacheri* was a total triumph.

More such triumphs followed. Next year, MS sang at the Kumbakonam Mahamaham (the 'Kumbh Mela' of the South) festival, where many other leading musicians also participated. The organisers had arranged a *kacheri* by Maharajapuram Viswanatha Iyer and presented him with a gold medal. The singer, who was present at the MS concert, was so overwhelmed by her singing, that he rushed to the dais and presented her with the same gold medal! "You deserve this award, you will be a great singer in the days to come," he said, blessing the shy young girl.

The public response to the MS *kacheri* was so great that a second programme had to be organised to satisfy the demands of the listeners. The well known Tamil film director, K Subramaniam, who was to play a significant role in MS's career, was in charge of the concert.

Shanmukhavadivu, delighted at her daughter's progress, knew it was now time to plan ahead. The family permanently shifted to Madras, where they rented a house in Puraswalkam and renewed contacts with Veena Dhanammal. She regularly performed at the Matunga Sangeeta Sabha in Bombay, and recommended Subbulakshmi for a concert. The young girl was in the company of stalwarts, as the programme included a concert by the famous

Brinda-Muktha-Abhiramisundari trio, and a dance recital by Balasaraswati.

There was a minor problem on the eve of MS's departure to Bombay. Violinist Mayavaram Govindaraja Pillai, who was to accompany MS, backed out at the last moment. A substitute could not be found, but the organisers were unwilling to disappoint thousands of Bombay fans who were keen on listening to MS. Finally, a local violinist was engaged. The concert was a smash hit. The male escort on Subbulaksmi's maiden trip to Bombay was a young man called T.Sadasivam, who undertook the responsibility despite a severe toothache. This young man was to play a major role in her future life.

Sadasivam in his twenties

CHAPTER THREE

Movies, Marriage and More Music

Even as M.S.Subbulakshmi was making waves in the Carnatic music world, India was in the throes of the freedom struggle. Following Gandhiji's footsteps, the rest of South India did not lag behind in demanding the departure of the British. Thiagarajan Sadasivam, a young man passionately devoted to the cause of *Swaraj*, travelled around the state, advocating the use of *khadi*. He sang patriotic songs at markets and thoroughfares, urging people to boycott and burn foreign textiles. Initially, Sadasivam favoured the extremist approach, even supporting the use of force in the freedom struggle.

But in 1924, after listening to Gandhiji at the Belgaum Congress session, the young man was won over to the path of *ahimsa* and became a follower of Gandhiji.

Despite being jailed thrice by the British, Sadasivam continued to propagate the use of *khadi* and market it successfully all over Tamil Nadu. This experience helped him in his job as the business manager of the successful Tamil weekly, *Ananda Vikatan*. The same Sadasivam accompanied MS on her first visit to Bombay and slowly his friendship with the MS family grew. He attended all her programmes and was thrilled at her progress in the music world. Sadasivam, however, felt that MS could reach greater heights if she planned her career more carefully.

MS, already a household name in Tamil Nadu, now had the choice to reach out for new horizons. Film director, K.Subramaniam, who had arranged her concerts at the Kumbakonam festival, was making a film based on a novel by well known Hindi writer, Munshi Premchand. Titled *Sevasadanam*, the film dealt with nationalistic ideals and revolutionary social themes. He needed a new face for the role of the film's heroine, Sumati. Subramaniam ran into MS at the home of the well-known Tamil actress, S.D.Subbulakshmi, who also had a role in his new film. "She is my Sumati, my heroine", exulted Subramaniam on seeing MS, and offered her the role.

The MS family knew the credentials of director Subramaniam and were happy with the film's theme. *Sevasadanam* was released in 1938. Any film featuring MS had to have songs, and this was no exception. The songs became hits, the records sold in thousands. MS was now flooded with offers from film producers. But the modest young woman was not keen on becoming the traditional film star. She was a singer and was happy with it. But she accepted the lead role in *Sakuntalai*, the immortal love story. Playing the role of King Dushyanta opposite her was another stalwart of Carnatic music, G.N.Balasubramaniam. Though GNB had no acting experience, he was selected only for his singing abilities.

Interestingly, *Sakuntalai* was directed by Ellis R.Dungan, an Ohio-born American who did not know any Tamil! A wizard with the movie camera, Dungan's skills helped in creating memorable scenes in *Sakuntalai*, like the one where angels come out dripping wet from a pond, and are seen soaring towards the sky. The 'angels' were fair-skinned local Anglo-Indian girls and the sequence was shot in the swimming pool of a local hotel. Dungan made the women wet their costumes and took shots of them jumping into the pond. Very cleverly, he then reversed the shot so that it showed

M.S. Subbulakshmi as Narada Muni in 'Savithri'

the girls soaring in the sky! No wonder, Dungan was a much-sought-after director. He and MS came together yet again in 1945 for *Meera*, the highpoint of her cinematic achievement.

Sakuntalai, released in 1940, was a major hit. Even today, people hum its popular songs, *Premayil Yavum Marandhome* (In our love, we forgot everything) and *Anandamen Solvene* (I would say it was happiness). The music duo of GNB and MS did not disappoint viewers. Essentially a musical, the film had some excellent visuals and, of course, the romance of *Sakuntalai* was well known.

Even while the films were being shot, Sadasivam had come closer to the MS family. Though married and a father of two daughters, Radha and Vijaya, he had fallen in love with the beautiful singer and she was not averse to his attentions. Mother Shanmukhavadivu, readily gave her consent to Sadasivam's marriage proposal. On July 10, 1940, at Tiruneermalai, a temple town near Madras, the couple were married in a simple ceremony. One of the key figures behind the happy event was K.Srinivasan, the editor of the popular daily, *The Hindu*.

More than MS herself, Sadasivam was aware of her potential, her genius. Having watched her music career closely, he was certain that MS could be a major figure in the world of music. She was a priceless but raw diamond which would dazzle after being polished. Endowed with a God-given voice and talent, she could unite the world, delight audiences and reach heights which no singer had scaled before. This was a challenge for Sadasivam. He felt his wife should be something more than just a singer. In fact, Sadasivam wanted MS to play a role in the National Movement and soon introduced her to leaders like Mahatma Gandhi, Rajagopalachari and Pandit Nehru.

Subbulakshmi as devotee Meera

But first it was the question of music. Sadasivam was keen that MS music should go beyond pleasing millions of fans. The music should reach higher levels and embrace God, be strongly focussed on *bhakti*. Music should elevate not only the senses, but also the

MS, the heroine of 'Sakuntalai'

soul. MS herself was a God-fearing woman and readily agreed to her husband's suggestions. She now began focusing more on the *bhakti* theme in her music.

Sadasivam had other ideas too. Despite possessing great voices, how many singers really understood the real meaning of the songs and communicated them flawlessly to the audiences? He strongly felt the need for clarity of expression, which was as important as *shruti* and *laya*. The audiences must understand every single word from the songs. If MS today is regarded as a symbol of national integration, one reason is that her repertoire included compositions in languages from many parts of India. This catholicity was consciously developed by Sadasivam who saw music not merely as an aesthetic exercise but as a vehicle for spreading spirituality among people.

'I love thee, O Lord!' From the film 'Meera'

Sadasivam and Subbulakshmi, when they were married in 1940, at Tiruneermalai

Under her husband's careful tutelage, MS continued her music lessons from stalwarts like Semmangudi Srinivasa Iyer, composer Papanasam Sivan, T.L.Venkatrama Iyer, Dwijendarlal Rai and Pandit Narayanrao Vyas. Benares-based Siddeshwari Devi taught her the nuances of Hindustani classical music while she learnt *bhajans* from Srinivasa Rao. The intricacies in singing *padams* and *javali* were explained to her by the well known singer, Brinda, the grand daughter of Veena Dhanammal. Inspired by her husband, MS also learnt to speak Telugu, Kannada, Hindi and Sanskrit.

Since MS was a willing learner, the results began to show. At a concert in Delhi, a Sikh admirer jumped up and exclaimed, "How can a South Indian sing such perfect Hindi songs?" For a performance in Calcutta, MS wanted to sing four *shlokas* from Kalidasa's *Mega Sandesam*. She requested the Sanskrit scholar, K.Chandrasekharan, to write down the four *shlokas* and their meaning in Tamil. The scholar was then invited to the rehearsals to spot mistakes.

It is now universally acknowledged that without curtailing her creativity in any way, Sadasivam, planned and perfected the music career of MS. Each concert was carefully planned, taking into consideration the venue and the tastes of the audience. While this strategist designed the format and all the numbers from the *varnam* to the *tukkadas* (lighter numbers), the combination of composers and languages, and the main and ancillary *ragas* for the evening, he also allotted the duration for each and every item.

Sadasivam and Subbulakshmi

Sadasivam sat in the first row in the auditorium and made signals to his wife which were not visible to others. The concert had to end even when the audience was thirsting for more! MS herself laid out and embellished the major pieces mentally, rehearsing constantly. Prior to the concert, during the rehearsal, Sadasivam posted men at different corners of the auditorium to test the acoustics and even checked the colours of the stage curtains. They had to match the mood of the concert!

It was true that Sadasivam did persuade her to act in certain films with specific financial objectives in mind. But he saw to it that they were idealistic movies with unforgettable music, like *Sakuntalai* and later, *Meera*.

Did MS, the creative artiste, ever feel uncomfortable at the initiative taken by Sadasivam in moulding her career? A traditional Hindu housewife, MS often referred to Sadasivam as her *'pathi dev'* and paid tributes to his role in developing her art. Calling her husband her 'friend, guide and philosopher', MS explained time and again, "I owe everything I have achieved to my husband. By his loving care, he is my parent; by his unerring guidance, he is my preceptor. He gave artistic shape and definition to my ideas on music which were almost running wild."

CHAPTER FOUR

The North Beckons

1940 was an important year for M.S. Subbulakshmi. *Sakuntalai* was a hit film, she got married and further laurels came her way. After a concert at Kumbakonam's prestigious Vani Vilasa Sabha, MS was honoured with the title, 'Isai Vani' and was now known as 'Kolila Gana Isai Vani' (melodious music queen). She became the most sought-after artiste and also the highest paid. Said noted musician Musiri Subramaniam Iyer, "Organisations which needed funds competed with one another to hold MS concerts".

At home, Sadasivam who was restless at the *Ananda Vikatan*,

Concert in Delhi attended by Jawaharlal Nehru, T T Krishnamachari, Babu Rajendra Prasad, Dr. Radhakrishnan and Indira Gandhi

finally resigned his job. So did the editor of the magazine and close friend, R.Krishnamurthy, popularly known as 'Kalki' , one of the most brilliant writers in Tamil. They wanted to start a new Tamil weekly called *Kalki*. The magazine needed funds and MS volunteered to help by acting in a film. This was *Savithri*, a mythological film where she played the role of sage Narad. As usual, the film was packed with songs. Since Madras lacked studio facilities, the film was shot at New Theatre Studio, Calcutta.

On their way to Calcutta, the Sadasivams broke journey at Nagpur to visit Gandhiji who was camping at Sewagram. They attended

Dilip Kumar Roy and Subbulakshmi

Gandhiji's prayer meetings. The Mahatma invited MS on stage to sing. Highly honoured, Subbulakshmi sang some devotional songs which thrilled the crowd. Gandhiji blessed her and promised to keep in touch.

Shooting for *Savithri* began in 1941. Though uncomfortable in her male costume for the role of Narad Muni, MS carried on bravely. One of the highlights of the film was the song *Bruhimuhun Deti* which was to become a hit. On the day of the song recording, MS was pleasantly surprised to receive visitors — well known singers, K.L.Saigal, Kanan Bala and Pahari Sanyal. They warmly congratulated the singer and wanted encores. Shanta Apte who played the role of Savithri in the film also became an MS fan. The film clicked at the box office, audiences wildly cheered the scene where Narad Muni descended from heaven singing the hit song and MS handed over her fee from the film to her husband to start *Kalki* magazine.

Both MS and Sadasivam were now keen to improve their contacts in the North. They readily accepted an invitation for MS to sing at the prestigious Vikramaditya Music Festival in Mumbai in 1943, patronised by leading Hindustani classical singers. MS excelled in her favourite *Sankarabaranam* raga. As the applause continued, MS was delighted to receive plaudits from Pandit Onkarnath Thakore, the doyen of North Indian classical music. Noted musician Bade Ghulam Ali Khan called her 'Suswaralakshmi Subbulakshmi'. Roshanara Begum, Pannalal Ghosh, Ravi Shankar, and Amir Khan conveyed their appreciation. The MS repertoire now contained several *bhajans* of Tulsidas, Meerabai, Kabir and Guru Nanak, which were tailormade for Hindi-speaking audiences.

"If there is radiance in the heart, there will be radiance in the music", MS often explained. It was the quality of emotion that she admired most in the music

A man she admired, Ustad Bade Ghulam Ali Khan

With Ravi Shankar, Lakshmi Shankar, Alla Rakha and Zakir Hussain

of Bade Ghulam Ali Khan. "What a moving, melting voice Khan
Saheb has!" she exclaimed once. "He puts his entire heart and soul
into his singing. I wish I had heard him earlier in my life." When
MS was informed that Hindustani singer Siddeshwari Devi admired
her, she replied modestly, "Siddeshwari Devi was an affectionate,
motherly personality. I was fortunate to have her as a guest in our
Madras home. That was the time when I learnt some *thumris* from
her." MS was unhappy that she could meet and exchange notes on
music with noted singer Begum Akhtar only towards the end of
the latter's career. This happened when the singer visited Madras

during a concert tour and was received by the Sadasivams. They presented her with a *Ponnadai* (gold brocade shawl)

The increasing number of *bhajans* in the MS concert stressed the *bhakti* element in her music. But while Paluskar, K.L. Saigal and other North Indian singers were avidly heard and appreciated in the South, its own singers had not been able to cross the geographical and musical boundaries. With the arrival of MS, these barriers began to fall. She conquered the North with her Meera *bhajans* which became a rage after the release of the Hindi version of the film.

The new-found interest in singing *bhajans* did not mean any neglect of Tamil songs. She was greatly helped by people like 'Kalki'. One of his songs, *Malai Pozhudinele* reached the peak of melody. Its incomparable sweetness and the beauty of its lyrics, made it one of her most popular renderings. According to South Indian tradition any young man who went to 'see' a girl for the purpose of matrimony, enquired if his would-be-bride was familiar with *Malai Pozhudinele* and would she please sing it!

While the 'conquest' of the North was heartwarming for MS, she was equally happy at the success of the *Kalki* which soon challenged the supremacy of *Ananda Vikatan*. The magazine brought a further benefit to the Sadasivams. The venerable Congress leader of Tamil Nadu who became the Governor-General of India, C.Rajagopalachari (Rajaji), took a keen interest in *Kalki* and became a family friend.

Rajaji shared the nation's grief at the death of Kasturba, Gandhiji's wife in 1944. The Congress was keen to raise suitable memorials for this remarkable woman who sacrificed everything for the sake of her husband's dream of an Independent India. Funds were needed. Rajaji thought that the highly popular concerts of Subbulakshmi could raise large amounts of money for the memorials. The Sadasivams agreed enthusiastically. Five concerts were organised at Madras, Tiruchi, Madurai, Coimbatore and Thanjavur for the Kasturba Memorial Fund. They were sellouts and money poured in. Gandhiji thanked MS and blessed her in a handwritten note, signing his name in Tamil. The note became a cherished possession of the couple.

The success of the MS concerts for charity inspired Sadasivam to another major decision. That MS would now sing only for charitable causes — religious, social and those aimed to promote education and alleviate the sufferings of the poor. The couple stuck steadfast to this decision and the collections from thousands of concerts and royalties from the sale of records and cassettes helped to complete major projects all over the country.

Later in her life, after receiving the Ramon Magsaysay Award, MS donated the entire amount to three organisations, the Bharatiya Vidya Bhavan (Bombay), Voluntary Health Services (Madras) and Raja Veda Pathashala (Kumbakonam). The royalties from the recordings of her devotional songs in ten different languages, also went to the Bhavans institution. The total donations from MS

With Alladiya Khan, the maestro of Hindustani music

concerts and sales of records and tapes, at a rough estimate, has exceeded Rs.2 crores over the years.

Next, Sadasivam was keen to make one more film with MS with the focus on music and *bhakti*. Several topics were discussed, 'Kalki' was consulted and finally the choice was made. MS would star in a film — based on the legend of Meera, the Rajput Queen who chose Lord Krishna as her husband. The legend was more popular in the North but had a universal appeal. MS agreed enthusiastically. Her stepdaughter, Radha, would play the young Meera. Ellis R.Dungan was to direct the film.

The film was extensively shot in locales in Jaipur, Udaipur, Chittor and Dwarka. The Maharana of Udaipur, the chief guest at an MS concert, was simply overwhelmed. When requested to loan some of his horses and elephants for the film's battle scenes, the Maharana promised all help. "Take what you want," he told Sadasivam, "The *Kalyani Raga* MS sang is still ringing in my ears. How can I deny her film anything?".

The film had great music, excellent performances and amazing camera work. Ellis R.Dungan realised that *Meera* was something special and made it a visually opulent film. The director, himself an excellent cameraman, and his cinematographer, Jiten Banerjee used a mould of MS's face and shot it at various angles again and again, with a variety of lighting techniques. After watching these shots for several hours, Dungan and Banerjee, chose the best to be used in the film to create what was later described as "Meera's ethereal, angelic beauty."

Another scene in the film where the young girl Meera changed into adulthood also created history. The transition was shown in a song sequence, 'Nanda Bala En Manala' where Radha and MS were featured. When the changeover took place, there was a 45-second fast-paced orchestra, a musical interlude as part of the song. Normally such musical interludes were also recorded along with the song in a recording studio long before the actual film shoot commenced.

Dungan tried a novel approach. He first shot the scene and the changeover sequence consisted of a number of shots of the statue of Lord Krishna, lighted lamps with flames flickering, flowers on plates and prayer offerings, Krishna's flute and then a cut to the close up of MS singing with great feeling and emotion, 'Hey! Murali.....Mohana...!'

There were no zoom lenses in those days. The shots were static and on fast trolley in close up. Dungan edited them himself into a rapidly cut, fast-paced sequence. Talented music director Venkataraman scored the background music in rhythm with the shots. It was the first time that such a technique was used and the impact was electrifying. It evokes admiration even today.

The success of the Tamil *Meera* in the South, prompted Sadasivam to attempt a Hindi version of the same film. The project took nearly one year, Radha and MS spoke their Hindi dialogues perfectly. *Meera* was released on December 5, 1947 at New Delhi's Plaza theatre. The invitees would make a 'who's who' on the Indian scene – the Governor General of India, Lord Mountbatten and his wife, Prime Minister Jawaharlal Nehru and his cabinet, and a host of other leading personalities. It was a difficult time for India. The newly-Independent nation was facing a military crisis in Kashmir though that did not deter the enthusiasm for *Meera*.

As the VIP guests trooped in, Nehru acted as the unofficial host and compere, and sitting next to the Mountbatten couple, explained to them the nuances of the film. Sarojini Naidu, the poetess known as the 'Nightingale of India', made a special appearance at the beginning of the film to introduce MS to the audiences. "I make the speech in English," explained Sarojini Naidu, "because I want to introduce MS not only to the Hindi-speaking North Indians, but to the entire world." After the film ended, Sarojini Naidu announced she was forfeiting her title as the 'Nightingale of India'. "Listen to the MS songs in the film, she is the one worthy of this title," Naidu announced.

With friend and admirer Sarojini Naidu

Meera was soon released in packed theatres all over India and broke box office records. The media raved over the film. The *Free Press Journal's* film critic wrote, "*Meera* transports us into a different world of *bhakti*, piety and melody. It shatters the misguided belief that film music is inferior. Subbulakshmi follows no stereotyped techniques in acting. She is just Meera." According to a New Delhi daily, any hardboiled atheist after watching *Meera* and listening to its songs would have a change of heart and become a Krishna worshipper!

The Meera *bhajans* also brought the MS family closer to Gandhiji.

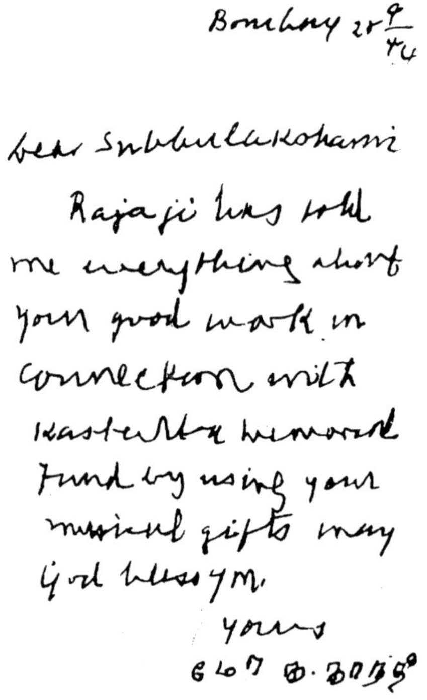

Bombay 28/9/46

Dear Subbulakshmi

Rajaji has told me everything about your good work in connection with Kasturba memorial Fund by using your musical gifts may God bless you.

yours
C. Rajagopalachari

Gandhiji's blessing

India, by now, was a free nation but Gandhiji was distressed at the spreading communal riots and tried hard to unite Hindus and Muslims. The Sadasivams visited Gandhiji during their Delhi trip for the release of *Meera* and found him downcast. There was some consolation when the Mahatma asked MS to sing the *Ram Dhun* at his prayer meeting. That proved to be her last meeting with Gandhiji.

MS was invited to sing some *bhajans* for Gandhiji's birthday on October 2, 1947. Unable to reach Delhi because of family problems, she recorded the *bhajans* and sent them to the capital. On October 1, MS received a message from Delhi that Gandhiji liked listening to the Meera *bhajan, Hari Tum Haro Janki Pir.* Unfortunately, MS was not familiar with this particular *bhajan* but how could she refuse Gandhiji, that too on his birthday! There was a further telephone call in the evening. If MS could not set tune to this *bhajan,* she could just recite it and send the recording.

At Gandhiji's prayer meeting at Wardha

This was a real challenge. Composers with their orchestra were urgently summoned and different tunes tried out. By midnight, the tune was finalised. Recording facilities in those days were available only in the studios of All India Radio. Rushing against time, the *bhajan* was sung and recorded at the Madras studio of All India Radio, and the recording despatched to Delhi by the morning flight. On the evening of October 2, the *bhajan* was played at the prayer meeting and moved everyone present.

On the evening of January 30, 1948, MS was at her home listening to a radio broadcast of the Thygaraja Music Festival from Thiruvaiaru. Suddenly there was an interruption followed by the sombre announcement that Gandhiji had been shot dead. This was followed by her own *bhajan, Hari Tum Haro.* Shocked to the core, MS fell down in a swoon. For weeks together, she moved around as though in a daze and tears kept pouring from her eyes.

CHAPTER FIVE

The Cultural Ambassador

Gandhiji was no more but his memory continued to haunt the Sadasivams. MS often recollected how she prepared herself to sing yet another of Bapu's favourite *bhajans, Vaishnava Janato*. Deeply moved by the *bhajan*, Gandhiji had once told Manu Gandhi, "Subbulakshmi, while singing, comes closer to God and the same happens to those who listened to her." The Sadasivams were further delighted when they purchased a bungalow located in Kilpauk, formerly owned by Justice Tyabji, where Gandhiji once stayed for ten days.

The void left in MS' life by the death of Gandhiji was partly filled by the love and affection shown by Jawaharlal Nehru. He never missed an MS concert in Delhi and at one of these observed, "What am I, an ordinary Prime Minister before this Queen of Music?" He went on to repeat these words at other public gatherings too where MS was present.

The Sadasivams stayed with the Prime Minister when they went to Delhi in 1953 for a concert for the Kamla Nehru Memorial Hospital. The Prime Minister was an attentive, at times a fussy host. At mealtimes, showing great concern, he would advise, "Subbulakshmi, don't eat this stuff, this is a bit too spicy. Keep away from very cold stuff, you must be careful about your throat!"

Pandit Nehru's daughter and future Prime Minister, Indira Gandhi, was equally attentive.

With Indira Gandhi

Laying the foundation stone for a students' hostel where MS had sung the prayer song, Indira Gandhi observed, "Why do you seek my blessings for this project? Any programme where MS has sung a prayer song is bound to succeed!"

The Indian Government also did not lag behind in officially honouring Subbulakshmi. The National Awards were instituted in 1954 and a grateful nation honoured MS with a Padma Bhushan. Eleven years later, she received the Padma Vibhushan and the highest of them all, the Bharat Ratna came in 1998.

MS was now a truly national figure and this was acknowledged when Lord Harwood and his wife, came to India and met the Sadasivams at their Madras home. After listening to MS, Lord Harwood, who was associated with the famous Edinburgh Cultural Festival which attracted the cream of western cultural talent, invited MS to perform there. She would sing at the festival on two days, August 30 and September 3, 1963.

This was Subbulakshmi's first musical performance outside India. It was a major challenge. Hardly anyone in the Western world was familiar with the complex Carnatic music system. North Indian music, particularly the instrumental variety, was slowly gaining popularity in the West, thanks to the efforts of sitarist Ravi Shankar

On her first foreign trip with husband,
Sadasivam, 1963

At the premiere of Meera *with Lord and Lady Mountbatten and Jawaharlal Nehru*

and tabla player, Alla Rakha. It was now left to MS to break the barrier against Carnatic music. Discussing the subject with Jawaharlal Nehru, Sadasivam observed that the West might prefer instrumental to Indian vocal music. "Yes" replied Panditji tapping his fingers on the table and then turning to MS, added "But not in YOUR case"

MS remembered these words as she sat down to perform at the Edinburgh Festival. The Western audiences were enchanted, the *Times* and other newspapers carried flattering write-ups, and MS participated at a BBC discussion on world music. After some more programmes in England and Europe, MS performed at Cairo.

In early 1966, she was thrilled to receive an invitation from UN Secretary General, U Thant, to perform at the UN General Assembly in New York. The spade work for the programme was done by senior UN bureaucrat, C.V.Narasimhan, a close family friend and a long standing admirer of MS. The UN concert was in October, 1966, on Vijayadasami day and needed careful preparation and planning. Former Army Chief of Staff, General Cariappa, suggested that considering the importance of the concert, MS should sing an English song. Rajaji, when consulted, agreed and himself wrote a song on the theme of world peace. It was set to music in Western idiom by Handel Manuel, a musician working for All India Radio, Madras.

In the presence of U Thant and a host of international celebrities, MS began her concert with the famous Ram *kirtana, Rama Nannu Browvara* and ended it with a benediction composed by the Seer of Kanchipuram, Paramacharya. The English song written by Rajaji was the penultimate number of the concert. The applause was thunderous. Following the UN concert, MS undertook a 7-week tour across the US, performing at 15 centres.

The Ramon Magsaysay Award for public service, presented to her in Manila

Having won the West, the opportunity to conquer the East came in 1974 when the Government of Philippines honoured her with the prestigious Ramon Magsaysay Award, often referred to as the 'Nobel Prize of the East'. The glittering function at Manila was presided over by President Ferdinand Marcos and the First Lady, Imelda. After Manila, MS performed at Tokyo, Osaka, Hongkong and Bangkok before returning to India.

In 1977, the concert tour was focussed on the east coast of the US but the major show was at New York's well-known Carnegie Hall.

A Doctorate, which she awaits to receive with Mother Teresa

Narasimhan was a bit apprehensive about the reactions of the hard-to-please music critic of the *New York Times*. His fears were groundless. The music critic wrote, "Subbulakshmi's vocal contribution transcends words. The cliché of 'the voice used as an instrument' never seemed more appropriate. It could fly flutteringly or carry on a lively dialogue with the accompanists. Subbulakshmi and her ensemble are a revelation to the Western ears. Their return can only be awaited with eagerness".

CHAPTER SIX

The Singer, The Person

Conquering the music world was not all that difficult for Subbulakshmi. But no matter where she sang, MS still felt there was no place like home. The feeling was mutual. India loved this musical genius. The Ravindra Bharati University of Calcutta honoured her with a Doctorate, Delhi and Shri Venkateshwara Universities followed suit. The Madras Music Academy, where MS came into the limelight at the age of 18, honoured her with the 'Sangeeta Kalanidhi' title.

MS' contribution to *bhakti* sangeet was further embellished with the release of three major records — *Venkatesa Suprapadham*, *Bhajagovindam* and *Shree Vishnu Sahasranamam* — all *shlokas*, recited in her mellifluous voice. These became favourites in every Hindu home and the mornings began with the chanting of these *shlokas*. The huge royalties from these records went to different charities.

'Honouring a Living Legend' was the heading of an editorial in *The Hindu* when the nation awarded the Bharat Ratna to Subbulakshmi in 1998. "She is a phenomenon, a virtuoso with a repertoire which literally spans the entire universe of Carnatic music. Her concerts have unfailingly transported listeners to a sublime mood of ecstasy and devotion as her sole approach to singing is strongly influenced by the spiritual *bhava* or mood of the *sahityas* or the compositions... It would be a serious error to describe MS only as a Carnatic musician. She has, practically over the past 50 years, transcended the confines of traditional Carnatic music concerts, by bringing in the grandeur of Hindustani music as well. Also, MS has been unerringly described as the cultural ambassador of India."

Even the hard-to-please Delhi-based music critic, Subbudu admitted — 'Is it possible to have a genuinely critical assessment of her

music?' MS sang in an era when Carnatic music was both traditional and innovative, when giants like Ariyakudi Ramanunja Iyengar, Maharajapuram Viswanatha Iyer, G.N.Balasubramaniam and Semmangudi Srinivasa Iyer laid down the norms for concerts. Also, when other music greats (women) like D.K.Pattamal, M.L.Vasanthakumari and N.C.Vasanthakokilam were very popular.

Each singer has her own areas of specialisation, though MS enjoyed certain clear advantages. Her beauty, for instance. With her slim and petite figure, creamy complexion, curly hair, lovely, dreamy eyes, she looked like one of those maidens from the Ajanta frescoes. Coming back to her voice, MS could sing the most embellished melodies, trill like a bird and yet be agile like a flute, gliding from one note to another with an originality, vivacity and felicity that became a hallmark of her musical genius.

Sulochana Rajendran, singer and music critic based in Mumbai explained that MS' voice remained exactly the same, year after year, concert after concert. "You could follow her singing, even sing with her because there were no deviations. The consistency was amazing but this led to very little innovation." This could be due to the rigid patterns laid out for the MS concerts by her husband.

There was scope for improvisation in Carnatic music.
M.L.Vasanthakumari improvised a lot, every time she sang a song,
it was different. Bala Murali Krishna also improvised but knew
where to draw the line. D.K.Pattamal displayed a little more
originality and her voice had a lot more *azhutham* (heaviness)
MS, on the other hand, was more predictable. Her *ragam, thanam,
pallavi* was judiciously chosen and performed. She was always
well prepared but never went overboard.

Some of her fans were disappointed that she often deviated from
singing songs in the pure Carnatic music tradition, by branching
out to more and more into *bhajans*. This was inevitable because
in her career, MS had to perform before cosmopolitan audiences.
Gandhiji, Nehru and North Indian music lovers wanted her to sing
more *bhajans*. And then, the screen *Meera* was expected to sing
bhajans! The connoisseur of pure Carnatic music had to put up
with these and other light classical numbers from MS.

What about the in-depth quality of her music? Of course it was
remarkable, otherwise MS could not have remained on top for so
many decades. MS devotion to her art was total, fortunately she
did not have to bother about anything else. There were few family
problems, her life was efficiently managed for her by Sadasivam,

Though known as a singer, MS is also an accomplished veena player like her mother

and all she had to do was sing. However, one can only wonder if MS ever felt that her creative wings were clipped, even slightly, by the 'excessive' career management by her husband. Did she ever want to fly on her own wings, choose her own songs for a concert? We can only speculate.

Yes, there were occasions when she sounded wistful and felt she could have gone for some innovation and performed better. When MS was at her peak in the 1960's, she effortlessly sang at a Delhi concert, the Papanasam Sivan composition, '*Naavukku Iniya Narayana Divya Naamam*' in *Mohana Ragam*. The *Raga Alapana* which followed was equally brilliant, but not her handling of the *swarams*. When this was pointed out to her by a diffident, young music critic, MS did not flare up. She acknowledged in private that on second thoughts, the *swarams* were a bit out of context.

In an MS concert, the spotlight had to be on her, expectedly. Good accompanists can inspire singers to perform better and occasionally steal their thunder. This never happened with MS because somehow or other, gifted violinists like T.N.Krishnan, Lalgudi Jayaraman and M.S.Gopalakrishnan, seldom performed with her. MS accompanists, barring exceptions like T.Chowdiah, were sober and predictable, never likely to divert attention from her.

Many people believed that Subbulakshmi was a natural genius, that her music was not as much cerebral as inspired. But the discerning listener knew how her music was crafted and polished, how it balanced the conscious and unconscious elements. MS once explained, "The *ragaswarupa* must be established at once. Don't keep the listener in suspense whether it is *Purvikalyani* or *Panthuvarali*. This difference must come through in the way you dwell on the notes common to both the *ragas*, even before the introduction of dissimilar notes. In *Shankarabharanam*, stress the *rishabha*, but in *Kalyani*, accent the *gandhara* quickly."

In six decades of singing, MS developed a unique style of her own. As a critic pointed out, this was not based on identifiable techniques of execution, but on the communication of a mood, of an ecstasy of emotion. What the ancient theoreticians called *rasadhvani*, when art became an experience of that ultimate bliss, within and without, both immanent and transcendent.

This was achieved through *auchitya* – a wide term which embraced contextual appropriateness, adaptation of parts to one another and to the whole, a fitness of things and poetic harmony. MS exemplified them all in her choice of *raga* and *sahitya*, balance of mood and technique, in her 'mike sense' and timing, and in the

The 'bhakti' feeling in her music was reflected in the personal life of MS

consonance she established with her accompanists and audience.

It is universally acknowledged that celebrities, crave for publicity and would do anything to get mentioned in the media. M.S.Subbulakshmi, however, guarded her private life and the persona behind the famous singer was known only to a few family members and friends. Sadasivam saw to it that the media had no access to her and MS was quite happy to let him handle the journalists, that too only on matters of music.

Yet, the audience, enchanted by her voice and mastery over music, wanted to know a bit more about their idol. MS, it was clear, stuck to the old world concept of a Hindu wife, subservient to the husband, remaining all the time in the background. In appearance and lifestyle, she remained a conservative. The long *pallavs* of her handloom cotton or silk sarees tucked around the waist, the flower-wreathed *kondai* (hairstyle), diamond-encrusted nose ring and earrings, glass bangles among the gold ones, the row of *kumkum* and *vibhuti* (holy ash) from many temples dotting the turmeric-washed forehead she was the epitome of traditional Hindu womanhood. MS never tried to appear younger than she was. Millions saw her as the embodiment of grace, compassion, consideration and slightly unworldly!

MS' grand-niece, Gowri Ramnarayan, evocatively recollects, "My childhooood memories of grand-aunt Kunjamma are of trailing behind her to the *tulasi maadam* in the garden. Fresh from her bath, in a swirl of silk, diamonds and perfume, her tranquil face framed by a riot of curls, she would draw the *kolam*, light the lamp and do the *puja* with elegance in every gesture. I was convinced that she was a celestial being, like Goddess Minakshi or Saint Andal of the legends. How else could she be so radiant? Or create music which thrilled you all over? Her sonorous voice calms troubled minds, lightens heavy hearts, and brings solace and upliftment."

At a concert in Ayalur in Tamil Nadu, attended by people from

surrounding villages, an aged, dust-streaked couple reached the venue late and requested for a couple of more songs. "We walked 30 miles in the heat to hear you sing and waited till the end to make our request" they said. The accompanists pointed out that it was past midnight and MS had already sung for more than three hours. But unwilling to disappoint the couple, she sang a few more songs with the same verve and enthusiasm as at the beginning of the concert.

MS displayed the same concern on a concert trip to Vishakapatanam. Heavy rains lashed the city, there was no way the concert could be held and she had to be back in Madras the next day. But how can a concert for the building of a Vigneshwara temple be cancelled? MS and Sadasivam agreed to spend one more day and complete the engagement.

Such compassion and consideration extended to everyone, particularly fellow musicians and composers. Papanasam Sivan, one of MS's favourite composers, was considerably upset when a song on which he had spent much time and effort, was rejected by a film producer. Impressed by the song, Sadasivam and MS invited their orchestra, asked Sivan to compose a tune, and the song was sung by MS herself. The song, *Nee Eerangayenil Pukaledu* in *Atana Ragam*, became hugely popular, and its records sold in thousands. MS made it a point to sing this song at every concert of hers.

One of the close observers of MS in private life was Kalki Kannan who left his Mayavaram home at the age of 14 to work for Sadasivam and came to be regarded as a family member. He worked in various capacities on the sets of *Meera*, learnt block making and printing for *Kalki* and then sold space successfully for the magazine. In between, he accompanied MS and Sadasivam on their tours within the country and abroad.

"Sadasivam Mama and MS Mami, in fact, arranged my marriage with Lakshmi," recollected Kannan. "The entire *Kalki* team was present. When we settled down at Matunga in Bombay, Mama and Mami were frequent visitors, at least four or five times a year for concerts." Every concert was meticulously prepared, pointed out Kannan. The rehearsals were always at the Kannan home. On the day of the concert, MS had a light meal, mostly 'idli and chutney'. Sadasivam was very much in charge.

The MS entourage was large with plenty of baggage. Friends of the couple often came along and once the concert was over, anyone who was around was invited home for dinner. "It was a tough job cooking for so many people," recollected Lakshmi Kannan. "But quite often, MS Mami brought her maid and cook along, and they were a big help."

The MS hospitality extended to everyone even at her own home. An autorickshaw driver, after dropping a guest and having a *darshan* of Subbulakshmi, was pleasantly surprised when the lady of the house enquired if he had eaten and invited him for a meal! She was always concerned with the welfare of the servants. Despite donating crores for various charities, MS hardly ever bothered about buying things for herself. "I don't recollect MS Mami going shopping to buy sarees or other stuff for herself," said Kannan. "She had small pieces of white cloth to wipe away excess *kaajal* from her eyes, and these were also used as handkerchiefs. Once, after finishing a concert in Hongkong, Mami's slipper was torn. She asked me to get it repaired and would not buy a new pair. I could not locate any cobblers and had to make some urgent makeshift repairs myself!" he laughed.

On MS' 50th birthday in 1965, the family presented her with gold bangles. India was then at war against Pakistan, and the government appealed for funds from the public. MS who was performing at a concert, at a signal from Sadasivam, quietly removed the cherished, newly-gifted bangles, and donated them to the war fund.

"She never thought of her own needs and was perfectly happy in the shadow of her husband," pointed out Kannan. Well known Bombay journalist, O.K. Joshee, once interviewed Sadasivam, with MS sitting demurely next to him. After she went inside for some work, Joshee asked if he could meet MS and was astounded to know that the person who sat quietly in the background, was the great singer. He rushed in to seek her blessings.

In his long association with MS, Kannan remembered her losing her temper just once: "Way back, during the shooting of *Meera,* one shot was tricky. It had to be repeated again and again. It was a blistering hot day and Mami was tired. I approached her with a cup of coffee but she shooed me off!" A diabetic patient for over 30 years, MS never allowed her health to affect her performances, taking special precautions on the eve of a concert.

What is the routine at the MS home, the 12 A Kotturpuram bungalow in Adyar, Chennai? An early riser, MS after her morning coffee and bath, spends time in the puja room before an early lunch. A nap, and then she meets dozens of people who come to seek her blessings. There is a light tiffin and coffee, as the meetings continue.

With their daughters

MS watches TV for sometime, particularly the Tamil news, then has dinner before turning in.

After the death of Sadasivam in 1997, MS wears only cotton sarees. But she still uses her favourite soap, *Pears* and her hair is never without another favourite, jasmine flowers. Not particular about food, she avoids heavy, oily things. Sweets, of course, are taboo because of her diabetic condition. Her daily routine is controlled by her maid of several years, Visalam, who is referred to, with some awe, as the 'Home Minister'. She takes care that MS does not over-exert herself.

Today, her frail health has disrupted most of her activities. Yet visitors are always welcome. Conversation with them is carried on in several languages! MS had never been fluent in English, yet conversed with foreign dignitaries. "She did not have to talk much," quipped Kalki Kannan. "Her presence and smile lit up the room. That was more than enough."

MS being MS, the political parties would have loved any kind of rapport with her. Prime Minister Atal Behari Vajpayee and Home Minister, L.K.Advani often dropped in for 'social visits', so did leaders from the local DMK and AIADMK. Just before the last Lok Sabha polls, the irrepressible Janata Party leader, Dr. Subramaniam Swamy, visited the MS home twice. He was contesting the election from Madurai and hinted that the very presence of MS at one of his poll meetings would boost his chances. And if she said a couple of good words about him, that would be better. The great singer was simply not interested.

What more can be said about her? She arouses devotion more than analytical scrutiny, despite her undoubted prowess in music. In a nation quick to canonise and deify, she was first transformed into a saint, then into a veena-holding Saraswati.

Towards the end of each recital, MS would sound the cymbals in deep concentration for the Rajaji hymn, *Kurai Onrum Illai* (I have no regrets). But while the magic of Subbulaxmi's voice is no longer heard at live performances, her musical legacy lives on. It will endure forever as will her image as a saintly person. A second Meerabai.

CHRONOLOGY

- Born on September 16, 1916 at Madurai
- Had more than 2,500 songs in her repertoire
- Married Sadasivam in a simple temple ceremony on July 10, 1940
- Starred in four films: *Sevasadanam (1938), Sakuntalai (1940), Savithri (1941)* and *Meera (1945; Hindi version 1947)*
- Death of her husband Sadasivam in 1977

• Bagged more than thirty national and international awards. Her awards and accolades include the prestigious Bharat Ratna, Ramon Magsaysay Award and Doctorates from five universities

• Subbulakshmi's highly-acclaimed concerts abroad include:

1963 — Edinburgh Festival of Arts
1966 — UN General Assembly Concert
1977 — Coast-coast singing tour of the US for fund-raising causes
1977 — New York Carnegie Hall Concert
1982 — Inaugural concert, Festival of Britain at the Royal Albert
            Hall before Queen Elizabeth II
1987 — Concert at Berlin Rachmaninoff Hall